Ian Botham

JULIA HOLT

Registered Charity No. 1003969

When Ian Botham retired
in July 1993 at the age of 37,
England lost
its greatest all-round cricketer.

He was a match winner.

People went to see him
because he was more than just a cricketer.
He is a show-business personality.

Football or Cricket?

At school,
Ian Botham was a very good
all-round sportsman.
He played football, cricket and badminton.

When he left school,
he almost became a full-time footballer.
For a time,
he played professional football
(for Scunthorpe)
in the winter,
and professional cricket
(for Somerset)
in the summer.

In the end he decided to stick to cricket.

Perhaps it was because
his father and mother
both played cricket.

Cricket

Botham was chosen to play
for England in 1977.
On his first day of Test cricket,
he took 5 Australian wickets.

He was an exciting player to watch,
fast and powerful.
He could bowl, bat and field.
People loved to see his magic
on the cricket pitch.

Above all, he was a showman –
a big man with a big personality
(other cricketers called him Guy the Gorilla!).

Botham was Man of the Match
in the 1979 Test
between England and India.

After the match,
he was stopped for speeding on the M1.
The police man
asked for his autograph,
and let him off!

Botham has played Test cricket
all over the world.
In 1981 he was captain
of the team that played
against the West Indies.

He became famous for quick scoring.
In one match,
against the Australians,
he scored 200 runs
in just 272 minutes.

In the 1981 Test,
England kept the Ashes
thanks to Botham's 118 runs.
In 1986, he was banned from playing
for two months
for smoking cannabis.
When he came back,
he broke Dennis Lillee's record
of 355 Test wickets.

He has broken many other records
in his career.

At the age of 23,
he had scored 1,000 Test runs
and taken 100 Test wickets.
He did this in only 21 Tests –
fewer than anyone else had ever done.

He was the first player ever
to score 100 runs and take 8 wickets
in one innings
in a Test match in 1978.

And he scored the fastest 100 runs
in 1982 and in 1985.

Now, at the end of his cricket career,
he holds a record
of more than 5,000 runs scored
and almost 400 wickets taken
in 102 Test matches.

Botham has earned more money in cricket
than any other player.

But he has also had 10 operations
for serious cricketing injuries.
He has so many metal plates in his body,
he sets off the alarms in airports.

His body is telling him to slow down.
But this will not stop him
from being a showman.

Life Outside Cricket

Ian Botham leads a full life
outside cricket.
In all things,
he works hard and plays hard.

He crashed two sports cars
in one day in 1982.

He has played baseball in America,
and football in Australia.

He writes books about his life.

He is captain of a team
on the BBC's popular programme
A Question Of Sport.

He has also been in a pantomime.

But he is most famous
for his charity walks.

He has raised a lot of money for charity
by walking
from the top of Britain
to the bottom,
and by walking over the Alps.

For all his work,
he was given the O.B.E. in 1992.

The Future

Ian Botham lives in North Yorkshire
with his wife Kathy,
his son and two daughters.

His son Liam is 16,
and a good cricket player.
Botham would love to play
in the same team as his son.

There will be more
Questions of Sport
for the BBC,
and more charity walks.

He is also planning a new book.

Ian Botham is not going to sit still.
He still has a will to win,
and whatever he does next,
he's sure to give it his best shot!